FIRST 15 LESSONS

BANJO

by Kristin Scott Benson

**Includes Audio
& Video Access**

T0071514

PLAYBACK+
Speed • Pitch • Balance • Loop

To access audio, video, and extra content visit:
www.halleonard.com/mylibrary

Enter Code
5213-1112-8844-3936

ISBN 978-1-5400-0301-0

HAL•LEONARD®

7777 W. BLUEMOUND RD. P.O. BOX 13819 MILWAUKEE, WI 53213

In Australia Contact:
Hal Leonard Australia Pty. Ltd.
4 Lentara Court
Cheltenham, Victoria, 3192 Australia
Email: ausadmin@halleonard.com.au

Visit Hal Leonard Online at
www.halleonard.com

POSTURE WHILE SITTING

Let the banjo rest in your lap, with the neck pointing up at about a 45 degree angle. Even if you don't intend to stand with your banjo, it's still beneficial to wear a strap while sitting. Banjos are notoriously heavy, so anything we can do to improve stability is an asset.

POSTURE WHILE STANDING

There are many preferences for strap length, but a good standard is to position the banjo so that your thumb on the right hand is level with your belly button.

For years, I tried to wear my strap over my right shoulder instead of my neck. I tried this because of seeing pictures of Earl Scruggs playing his banjo this way, especially early in his career. Though I rarely do it, I am going to recommend deviating from his standard and suggest wearing your strap over your head, on the left shoulder. Also, wearing a wider strap helps the weight distribution, which is important, considering how heavy banjos can be.

THE LEFT HAND

Your left hand should help provide stability for the neck, but it doesn't need to grip or wrap around the neck with pressure. In general, our left hand rests loosely on the neck, with our thumb loosely wrapped around. There should be some clearance between the neck of the banjo and the arch of your thumb. Don't grip the neck like a baseball bat.

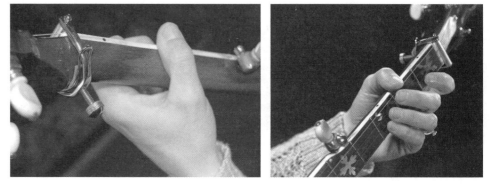

Sometimes, we intentionally move our thumb downward and place the thumb against the back of the neck, as if you're giving a thumb-print. This is especially useful when we play a more advanced style called single-string. For now, though, let's keep our thumb loosely wrapped, pointed upward toward the ceiling, with clearance between it and the neck.

The left-hand fingers should hover above the strings, close to them. We will continually emphasize efficiency throughout the book, and we want our fingers to be ready for action at all times.

Everyone has to figure out what works best for them with regard to hand positions. Feel free to experiment.

THE RIGHT HAND
One vs. Two Fingers Down

The most commonly asked question I hear from beginners is, "Do I have to anchor both my ring and pinky fingers on the head?" Again, Earl Scruggs, the father of three-finger-style banjo playing, anchored both. As a result, I recommend students try this approach, but I also quickly point out that there are many wonderful, professional banjo players who have only one finger anchored on the head. So, I encourage students to try planting both fingers, but as long as either of the fingers is planted (ring or pinky), you can proceed without much concern. I started by only planting my pinky on the head, but filed away the goal of having the ring finger also being planted. I didn't let this detail stall my learning or steal my joy, but noticed that after two or three months into the process, my ring finger had joined the pinky. It is crucial to remember this, however: in three-finger, bluegrass, Scruggs-style playing, at least one finger (pinky or ring) absolutely must be planted on the head.

Location of the Anchored Finger(s)

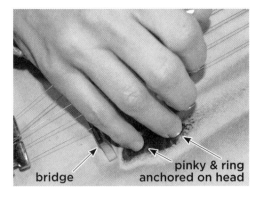

bridge | pinky & ring anchored on head

Our default right-hand location should be just in front of the bridge. Many people hook their pinky on the curve of the bridge. This can deaden the sound of the banjo, even though you might not be able to tell a difference yet. Let's just go ahead and get in the habit of planting the pinky just in front of the bridge. If you only plant the ring, it should be positioned where it would hit if the pinky were planted in this location.

As we begin playing up the neck, our right-hand location will change. In general, your two hands get closer together as your left hand moves up the neck. So, if you're way up the neck, near the 21st fret, your right hand will be on the head very near the fretboard. For now, however, let's stay close to the bridge, unless otherwise noted.

Putting on Your Picks

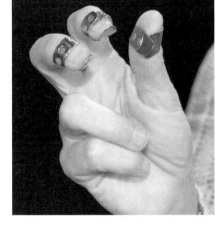

I recommend metal finger picks (for the index and middle) and a plastic thumb pick. Blue Chip makes a wonderful thumb pick that uses proprietary material for the blade, and you may want to eventually consider investing in one.

As with many aspects of banjo playing, there are several preferences on how to wear and position your finger picks. I suggest starting by letting your finger rest in the bottom bed of the metal pick, so that the blade curves naturally with the contour of your finger. Then, squeeze the bands until the picks are tight enough not to fall off, but not so tight that it will make imprints on your skin. The plastic thumb pick should fit snugly enough that it doesn't slide around, but not so tight that it cuts off circulation.

Default/Resting Position

With at least one finger anchored on the head, let your remaining fingers hover above the following: thumb over the third string, index over the second, and middle above the first.

In order to maximize efficiency, we must minimize motion. Think of a great typist. Their fingers stay on the home row keys. The fingers leave to strike the desired key, but then quickly return to their designated, default/resting position, hovering above their assigned home row keys. We will take a similar approach to our right hand. Each finger hovers above the assigned home-base string and leaves to strike the desired string with a controlled, intentional motion, minimizing movement. Wasted movement in the right hand will forever plague your playing, so it's smart to establish this good habit from the start, while you are concentrating on only a few things. Once you're playing songs and worrying about tons of details, it's easy to let this slide, but it's so important! Hold yourself accountable from the very beginning by asking, "Am I being efficient with my right hand?"

In general, our thumb plays the second, third, fourth, and fifth strings, our index plays the second and third, and the middle only plays the first.

TUNING

The standard tuning for the banjo—also known as "open G" or simply "G" tuning—is, from string 5 (the short string) to string 1 (closest to the floor): G–D–G–B–D.

Now, strum the banjo with your thumb, letting your anchored fingers leave the head and move with the rest of your hand. Congratulations! You just played your first chord: a G major.

A free online tuner comes with this book! Simply visit **www.halleonard.com/mylibrary** and enter the code found on page 1 to access it.

Before we learn our first roll, let's talk about some right-hand essentials. In bluegrass banjo playing, the right hand is everything. Quintessential masters of the five-string all have some common characteristics, and a precise right hand is at the top of the list.

No one can conquer all of these techniques at first. I encourage people to file these points away and spend part of the day concentrating on them, playing only simple rolls, even after you are moving into the intermediate or advanced stages of your playing. You shouldn't, however, let these details drive you crazy and stall your progress.

When you're focusing on the many details of playing a song (where does my left hand go? Which roll is next? I always miss this next part!), it's easy to let these fundamentals slide. That's understandable. Just make yourself aware of these goals and try to maintain an awareness of them while learning. After you have memorized a song, focus hard on making it sound good by applying these right-hand techniques.

RIGHT-HAND ESSENTIALS
Pick Direction

We want our fingers to strike the strings so that our picks hit as squarely as possible, in the center. Think of it as two parallel surfaces meeting.

No Bendy Thumb

Some people's thumbs naturally bend upward at the middle knuckle, creating a somewhat double-jointed arch. Others, when bent, form a straight line. Either works great. We want the thumb completely extended and the middle knuckle locked, wherever that may be. We want to avoid bending the outward knuckle down toward the strings.

Maximize Efficiency

We also want to minimize motion. Remember our resting/default right-hand position from Lesson 1? Wasted motion can prevent you from ever playing fast. We don't want our fingers flailing all over the place. Controlled, concise, and efficient— that's what creates accuracy, and it's absolutely crucial in bluegrass banjo playing.

Volume

Most people have a strong and/or weak finger(s). At first, try to make each note the same volume. Though we will want to syncopate our playing at times—i.e., accent some notes by making them louder—we want to solidify the ability to play uniformly first.

No Loping

As I just mentioned, syncopation is a valuable tool, whether it's done by accenting notes rhythmically or using volume. Certain songs and styles rely upon it, but in my experience, people who develop the habit of "loping" early on have a very hard time shedding it, even when they wish they could. So, let's concentrate on making the time between notes as consistent as possible.

This intentional effort is what gives us the machine gun-like precision that Earl Scruggs established as the precedent back in the 1940s. Setting a metronome at a low tempo—say 80 bpm—and playing one note of the roll per one click is a good way to ensure that you aren't letting the rhythm of your roll become erratic. It may sound more musical at first to lope, but our goal of achieving a somewhat monotonous uniformity is essential to creating a smooth, flowing sound later on.

A free online metronome comes with this book! Simply visit **www.halleonard.com/mylibrary** and enter the code found on page 1 to access it.

BEGINNING ROLLS – IT'S TIME TO PLAY!

Now, with everything that we've talked about so far in mind, let's get in our default/resting position. It's time to play our first rolls. Some people find it valuable to say the number of the strings, "3-2-5-1," as they play. Remember, the fifth string is the short one, so that immediately tells you the first is nearest to the floor.

> ## Tablature
> The notation system we're using here is called *tablature*, or *tab* for short. It's very easy to read. There are five horizontal lines on a staff that represent the five strings of the banjo. String 5 is on bottom, and string 1 is on top. The numbers on the lines tell you which fret to play on which string. A zero (0) indicates an open string.

The Alternating Thumb Roll: 3-2-5-1 & 4-2-5-1

This roll is aptly named because our thumb plays every other note. Before we get going, let's make sure we're up to speed with notation conventions. As will be the case with most examples in this book, this example is in *4/4 time*, which means there are four notes in a *measure* (the music staff is divided into measures by vertical lines), and a *quarter note* is counted as one beat. In other words, a quarter note lasts for one beat in 4/4 time. So when you count along with the beat, "1, 2, 3, 4," you're counting quarter notes. In the music, a quarter note is represented by a number on the staff with a stem hanging down from it.

The typical banjo roll, however, uses *eighth notes*, which last half as long as quarter notes. There are eight eighth notes in a measure of 4/4, and we count them as "1 & 2 & 3 & 4 &." So eighth notes are played twice as fast as quarter notes. In the music, their stems will be connected by *beams* when they're grouped together, or the stem will have a flag when an eighth note appears by itself. The "t" (thumb), "i" (index), and "m" (middle) letters below the staff represent right-hand fingering. The ||: and :|| symbols are called *repeat signs*, and they tell you to play the music contained within them again.

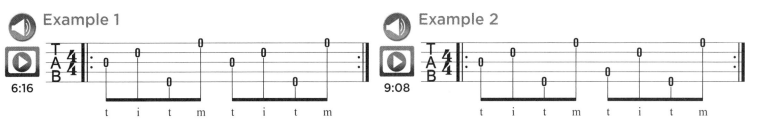

Example 1 — 6:16

Example 2 — 9:08

Forward/Backward Roll: 3-2-1-5, 1-2-3-1

You may have heard people talk about forward or backward rolls, which refer to the directionality of the strings being played. It doesn't imply a specific string order, only the direction your fingers are moving.

Think about falling forward, down, toward the floor. Fingers moving in this direction are creating a *forward roll*. We typically cycle back to our fifth string once we've run out of strings. Then, imagine someone grabs you by the collar, and you're being pulled back up toward the ceiling. Fingers moving in this direction are creating a *backward roll*. We oftentimes cycle back to the first string once we're done rolling toward the ceiling.

So, this roll includes both motions. The first section, 3-2-1-5, is forward, moving toward the floor and then on to the fifth string. The second section, 1-2-3-1, is backward, moving toward the ceiling and then back to the first string—hence the name.

Example 3 — 12:04

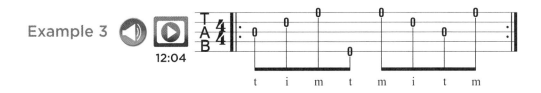

In Lesson 1, we talked about posture and having a relaxed left hand. Many people have to experiment to find the best way to fret notes. You have to make sure there is no buzzing and enough arch for open strings to remain open.

We want to fret each note close to the fret wire—not in the middle of the fret. Use just enough pressure so that the note does not buzz. We don't want to unnecessarily fatigue our left hand by pressing down too hard.

Your banjo's *action* (the distance between your fretboard and the strings) greatly affects playability. Making sure your instrument doesn't have excessively high action can ensure you are successful and not frustrated. In general, you should not be able to slide your pinky finger between the fretboard and strings, even at the highest point of action (usually where the neck meets the head of the banjo).

FIRST CHORDS: G, Em, C, AND D7

G Major Chord

The banjo is naturally tuned to an open G, so if you strum the banjo with nothing fretted, you're playing a G major chord. The chord symbol for a major chord is simply an uppercase letter. So "G" indicates a G major chord.

Chord Grids

A *chord grid* is a way to show chord fingerings on the banjo. Think of how a banjo looks when hanging on a wall in front of you; this is the way chord grids are oriented. String 1 is to the right, and string 4 is to the left. We don't often include the fifth string in a chord grid, because chord grips usually only include strings 4–1. The chord grid for the G chord tells you to play all five strings open. In other chords, dots will appear on the neck indicating a note should be fretted on that string. Numbers below the grid indicate the left-hand fingers used to play those fretted notes.

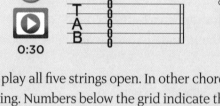

E Minor Chord

The chord symbol for a minor chord adds a lowercase "m" suffix to the uppercase letter. So "Em" indicates an E minor chord.

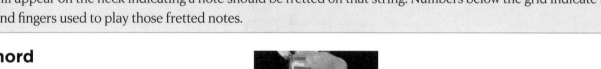

C Major Chord

D Dominant Seventh Chord

The chord symbol for a dominant seventh chord adds a "7" suffix to the uppercase letter. So "D7" indicates a D dominant seventh chord.

COMBINING CHORDS WITH ROLLS

Now, we get to pair the open rolls we learned in Lesson 2 with the chords from this lesson. I cannot overemphasize the importance of a strong right hand, so make sure you have made some progress on accomplishing good technique with the open rolls before adding these chords with the left hand. Your focus will inevitably be on the left hand once you add it, but don't forget all the essentials we talked about in the last lesson for the right hand. They still apply—and will forever more!

We are simply going to play each roll two times for each chord, cycling through G, Em, C, and D7. After you get the hang of it, use the guitar-only play-along track to practice by yourself.

Chords and the Alternating Thumb Roll, with Fourth String: 3-2-5-1, 4-2-5-1

In the last measure, you'll see several curved lines connecting four quarter notes. These are called *ties*, and they tell you to sustain the notes as one long note. So, since there are four quarter notes tied together, you'll sustain that open G string for four beats.

Example 1

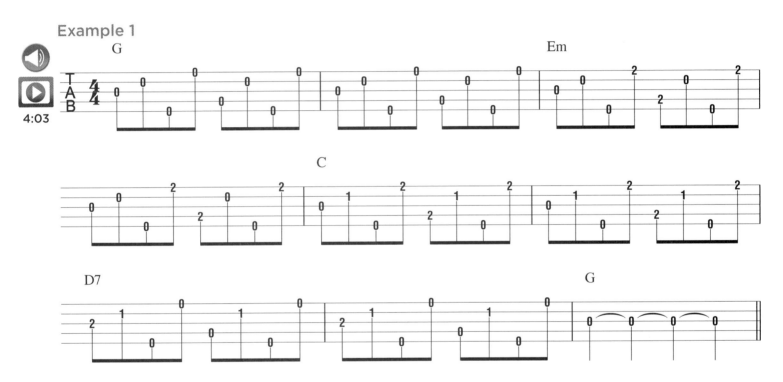

Chords and the Forward/Backward Roll: 3-2-1-5, 1-2-3-1

Example 2

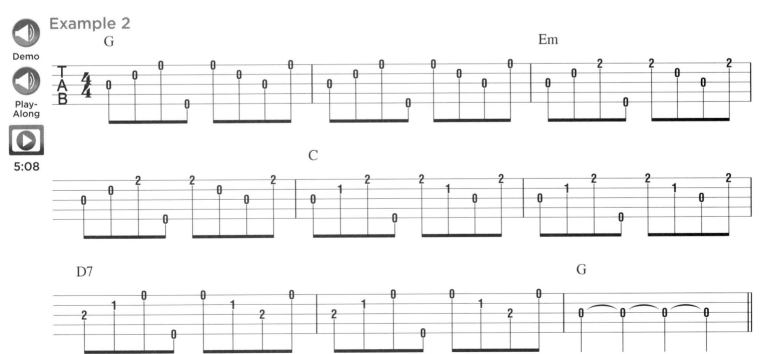

LESSON 4

 There are four basic left-hand techniques: *slides*, *hammer-ons*, *pull-offs*, and *bends*. For now, we are going to talk about the first three.

The goal of any left-hand technique is to make multiple notes sound by only striking the string one time with your right hand. Each note should be equal in value, volume, and prominence, which will take practice.

SLIDES

Place your left-hand middle finger on the second fret of the third string. Use your right-hand thumb to strike the string and then slide the left-hand finger to the fourth fret.

> ### Slide Tips!
> - Don't rush the slide. There is a designated timing to it.
> - Don't press so hard that it sounds like three separate notes (second fret, third fret, fourth fret). We want a smooth slur.
> - Use enough pressure or the note will die out during the slide.

In the music, a slide is shown as a diagonal line connecting two notes with a curved slur above it, which looks like a tie, along with an "s" above the slur. (In the following instance, since the destination note is tied to other notes, the slur extends across all the tied notes. Otherwise, it will extend only across the beginning and ending of the slide.)

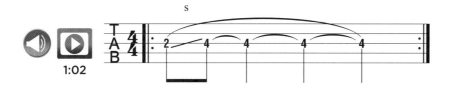

1:02

Note: eventually, we'll more likely slide only from the second to the third fret, but while we're learning how to slide, it's more gratifying to our ears to hear the fourth-fret resolution. We can also slide down in pitch (to a lower fret).

HAMMER-ONS

Hammer-ons are another way to smoothly ascend in pitch on one string. They can involve an open string and a fretted note or two fretted notes.

Take your middle finger on the left hand and let it hover above the second fret of the fourth string (but don't touch the string). Strike the open fourth string with your right-hand thumb and then press down quickly and firmly with your left-hand middle finger on the second fret. You should hear two notes: the open plucked fourth string and the second note, which was produced by the hammer-on (not plucked).

Hammer-On Tips!

- Don't rush the hammer-on. As with the slide, there's a designated timing to it.
- Maintain enough pressure to create sustain for the second (hammered) note.
- Don't be in a hurry to remove the hammered note because it robs it of its prominence.

In the music, a hammer-on is indicated by a slur (curved line) with an "h" above it.

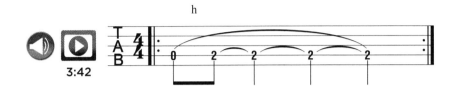

PULL-OFFS

Pull-offs are, by far, the most difficult left-hand technique. I heard Bill Evans, a wonderful banjo player/instructor/writer, joke that, oftentimes, the quality of your pull-off determines your pay-scale as a professional banjo player. He's not wrong! Perfecting this technique is a lifelong pursuit in and of itself. Don't let bad pull-offs stall your progress, but don't let them slide either—pun intended. Regardless of how frustrating it is, make yourself continually attend to the details of good pull-offs and do not take shortcuts. This is an essential element of good playing.

With your left hand, place your middle finger on fret 3 of the third string and place your index finger right behind it at fret 2 of the same string. Now, you're ready for action. Use your thumb to strike the third string, so you hear the third fret note. While the note is still ringing, swiftly pull the middle finger straight down or push it straight up off the string. This should make the second fret note (fretted by the index finger) sound. You're essentially "plucking" the string with the middle finger of your left hand. It will take practice! Don't get discouraged! This is one of the hardest things you'll ever learn.

Pull-Off Tips!

- As with the other techniques, don't pull off too fast. Also, don't rush to get the index out of the way after the pull-off is complete.
- Don't let your middle finger fly out away from the neck. It should move up or down, staying parallel to the neck and close to the strings.
- Both left-hand fingers must be fretted at the same time. Planting the index finger after you've already fretted with your middle will weaken your pull-offs.

In the music, a pull-off is indicated with a slur and a "p" above it.

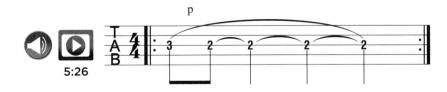

 Once you've spent time practicing slides, hammer-ons, and pull-offs by themselves, we can add a roll.

SLIDING WITH THE 3-2-5-1 ALTERNATING THUMB ROLL

Practice your open 3-2-5-1 alternating thumb roll again. You should be pretty good at this one by now. Once you have it at the forefront of your mind, add the slide we just learned to the first note, remembering all the goals we talked about.

In the last lesson, we slid from the second fret to the fourth fret on string 3. This is always acceptable. When combined with a roll, however, it's more common to slide from fret 2 to fret 3. So, we'll now hear what the slide technique sounds like when added to a roll and ending on the third fret. From this point forward, think of the 2-3 slide and 2-4 slide as synonyms. They are interchangeable, and it's your choice when to use which. Regardless of what's tabbed, you have the discretion. You'll see and hear it both ways throughout this book and when listening to other banjo players, in general.

> **Tips!**
> - Remember that there is a timing to the slide. Don't rush it.
> - The cadence, or timing, of the roll stays the same. Realize that your right hand should do the exact same thing, even though the slide has been added. There is no delay between the first two notes that you pluck.
> - Remove your middle finger as you strike the open fifth string to create the desired amount of sustain from the slide.

You'll also notice a new rhythm here: the *16th note*. These look like eighth notes but with a second beam. As you may have suspected, there are 16 16th notes in a measure, and they are twice as fast as eighth notes.

Example 1   2:02

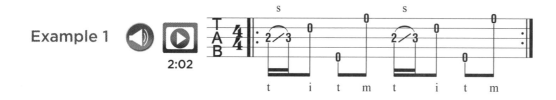

PULLING OFF WITH A NEW ALTERNATING THUMB ROLL: 3-2-3-1

This 3-2-3-1 sequence is new. Practice this pattern with open strings until you're comfortable.

Now, to add the pull-off, place both left-hand fingers (middle and index) down at the same time on their respective third-string frets. Strike the third string with your thumb and pull the middle finger straight down (or push it straight up).

> **Tips!**
> - As with the slide, remember that the timing of your right hand does not change. The pull-off happens within the roll. Don't rush the pull-off or delay the roll because of it.
> - Remove the index finger on the left hand from the second fret right before you strike the open third string. This allows the needed sustain from the second note of the pull-off.

Example 2   3:41

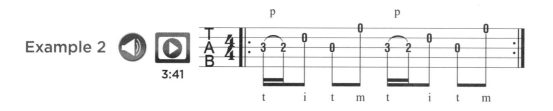

HAMMERING ON WITH THE 4-2-5-1 ALTERNATING THUMB ROLL

Practice the open roll 4-2-5-1 sequence again. Once you're comfortable, let your left-hand middle finger hover above the second fret of the fourth string. As you strike the fourth with your thumb, hammer on to the second fret.

> **Tips!**
> - Are you seeing a pattern? Maintain the timing of the open roll even after the hammer-on is added and don't fret the hammer-on too quickly.
> - Remove the middle finger as you strike the fifth string to retain the sustain of the hammer-on.

Example 3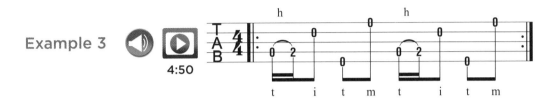

COMBINING ALL THREE TECHNIQUES

Now, let's play an exercise with all three left-hand techniques! Notice that we have a 5-1 pinch at the end. A *pinch* is just two or more strings struck at the same time. In this case, we're pinching the fifth and first strings together with our thumb and middle fingers, respectively.

Example 4

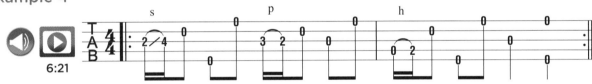

"CRIPPLE CREEK"

You just conquered 50% of the solo for the song, "Cripple Creek!" Let's make this our first tune. I'll shade the verbatim parts so you can see the repetition. In fact, the first phrase of the B section will be very simple too, since it's just the slide exercise played three times in a row, with an open fourth string, followed by a 5-1 pinch.

Notice that we'll play each part two times because of the repeat signs. Once you're comfortable, use the play-along track to practice by yourself with the guitar.

Example 5

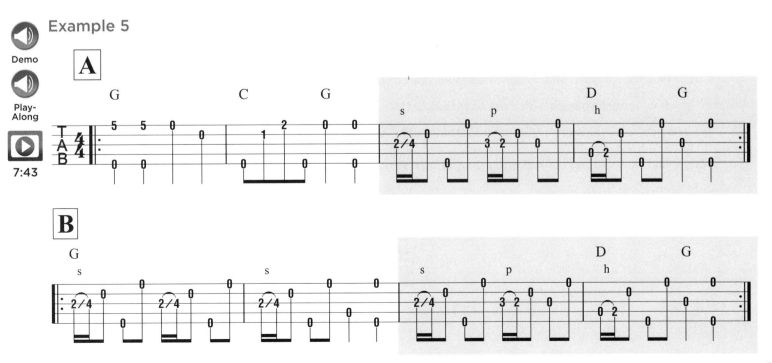

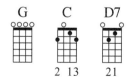 Almost every student I encounter seems mystified by the subject of *backup*. I've even met some folks who know solos to 20 or 30 songs but can't play backup to a single one. It seems to be an intimidating part of playing the banjo and oftentimes takes a back seat to learning solos. This is why I think we should lift the veil and tackle backup from the beginning.

First, let's talk about the importance of backup. During a typical song, you may play one or two solos, roughly amounting to 20 or 30 seconds. What are you going to do for the other two minutes while others play solos and the vocalists sing? Back them up! In fact, we will end up playing backup 80-90% of the time, yet many students (and teachers alike) give backup very little attention. My experience is that if we make backup a priority from the start, it's just a natural part of the learning process that accompanies learning solos. Frankly, until you can play backup, you haven't fully learned a song.

THE ROLE OF BACKUP

In general, there are three ways we play backup on banjo: low-rolling, vamping/chopping, and up the neck. In this book, we'll talk about the first two styles.

Every instrument in a bluegrass band has a job. Together, they create the basic rhythmic machine. The bass provides the downbeat, the mandolin provides the upbeat, the guitar fills in the gaps by strumming, and, unless we are vamping/ chopping (covered in Lesson 8), we provide the punctuated roll that subdivides the beats. The banjo is responsible for much of the momentum you hear in a bluegrass band, and that's what attracted me to the instrument as a child.

Backup is not hard. But isn't easy either. Let me explain.

It would be warranted to devote several books to this one topic. We can apply layer after layer of knowledge, creating in-depth and complex backup passages. At its most basic level, however, our job with backup is simply to play behind a singer or soloist in a way that complements them and doesn't distract listeners from what they are doing.

I have found the easiest way to accomplish this goal is by playing simple rolls low on the neck (near the tuners). The difficulty level is very low, and it should be easier than playing lead breaks. If we emphasize backup from the beginning, it prevents psychological barriers that possibly result from having avoided it early in our learning.

To summarize, while we could spend a lifetime studying the masterful backup skills of players like Earl Scruggs, Sonny Osborne, JD Crowe, and many others, we can fulfill our obligation as a backup player rather easily by taking the following approach.

LOW-ROLLING BACKUP TO "CRIPPLE CREEK"

Here is a basic strategy. Use a simple roll that you are good at—say the 3-2-5-1 alternating thumb roll—and play it over and over, making sure your left hand is fretting the appropriate chord. Let's tackle backup to "Cripple Creek" this way.

1. Play the roll open first, to be comfortable, before you add the chords.
2. Now, refresh yourself with these chords: G, C, D7

Note: We can play the more easily fingered D7 instead of a D chord anytime.

Notice that we try to end backup with a quarter note so that all your left-hand fingers are free to begin the solo.

Here are the chords we'll need.

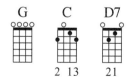

And here's a simple chord chart for "Cripple Creek."

Now here's what it looks like when we apply the 3-2-5-1 roll to the chords.

Example 1

Demo

Play-Along

6:55

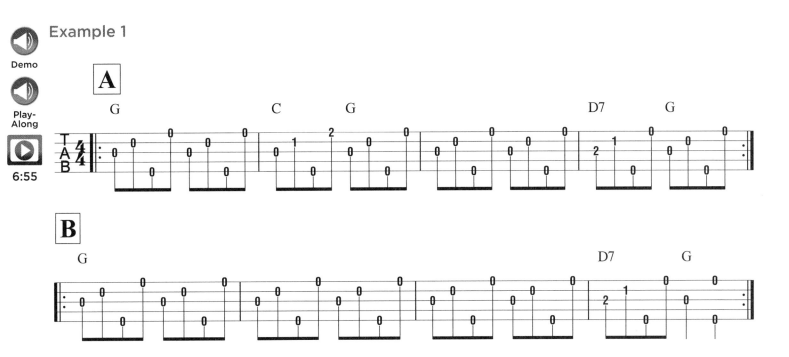

The goal of any musician is to be able to play lead and backup to every song. Play along with the previous full-band track to practice both. Here's how the track is laid out:

- The banjo will play a solo (Example 5 from Lesson 5).

- Then the banjo will play the backup (Example 1 above) during the guitar solo.

- Then the banjo will play the solo again.

This way, you can transition from lead to backup and then back to lead.

When you were a kid, did you like broccoli? How about asparagus? Spinach? Friends, consider Lessons 7, 8, and 9 the banjo equivalent of eating your vegetables.

While these topics may not be the most fun or immediately gratifying, they are crucial. If you'll devote the necessary time to them, I promise it will be worth it. In Lesson 10, we'll have dessert to make up for some of this hard work, so look forward to that.

In Lesson 6, we talked about the role of the banjo in backup and covered the most commonly used technique: low-rolling backup. The other topic we will cover in this book is *vamping*, or *chopping*. This is when the banjo creates a percussive sound, similar to a mandolin chop, on the upbeat.

Chopping requires closed-position chords, which means there are no open strings (with the exception of the fifth string, which is almost always open). So first, before we discuss vamping in detail in Lesson 9, we must first learn our closed-position chord shapes (this lesson) and understand how to move them around on the neck (next lesson).

For players who struggle with the left hand, fingering these chords can be quite a challenge. Please give it time and really commit to learning these positions, even if it feels awkward at first. Many people find that what seemed to be an insurmountable challenge eventually falls into place, and closed-position chords become a valued part of their playing. They aren't just used for backup. Solos rely heavily on up-the-neck chords, eventually, though we rarely use all four fingers while playing lead.

It's very important, even if you struggle to make these chord shapes, to understand the process of moving them around the neck because it gives us a basic understanding of the fretboard.

THE THREE MAJOR CHORD SHAPES

There are three major chord shapes (or positioning of your left-hand fingers) on the banjo. The most common ways to refer to them are the F-shape, the D-shape, and the barre-shape. We are going to use a G chord to demonstrate all three shapes.

Please understand that all of these are G chords! The shape changes (an F-shape, D-shape, barre-shape), but they are still all G major chords.

Practice fingering each of the shapes by simply strumming them with your thumb one string at a time. This helps to confirm you are cleanly fingering each note. Again, don't get discouraged. This may take some time. The quantity of work in this lesson is minimized to give you time to focus on fingering these challenging chords.

G Chord: F-Shape

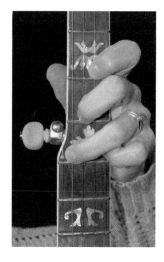

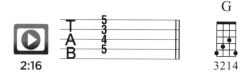

2:16

G

3214

G Chord: D-Shape

4:06

G Chord: Barre-Shape

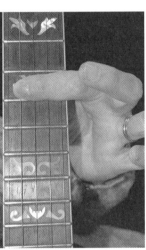

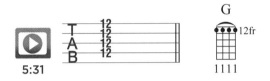

5:31

Note: There are many ways to finger a barre shape. This is only one of them.

🔊 Listen to the audio track to hear each chord form strummed twice.

SLIDING BETWEEN F-SHAPE AND D-SHAPE G CHORDS

A very worthwhile exercise is learning to shift between the F shape and D shape, which are the two most common positions, while chopping. Though we can chop in a barre shape, it doesn't happen as often.

Before we introduce the right hand into the equation, let's go ahead and tackle transitioning between the F and D shapes with our G chord, simply strumming down the banjo with our thumb.

> **Tip!**
> It's very important to keep your pinky and ring fingers in place. Don't lift them, but rather slide them back and forth. Then, the only fingers that have to be lifted are the index and middle fingers, which swap strings.

We also get our first look at a *rest* in this example. This symbol (𝄽) is a quarter rest, and it tells you to be quiet—i.e., "rest," or not play—for one beat. For every type of rhythmic note (quarter note, eighth note, etc.), there's a corresponding rest.

6:54

THE CHROMATIC SCALE

 Now that you have tried fingering each of the three major chord shapes, let's talk about the *chromatic scale*. It consists of 12 notes, and these are the only notes we'll ever use. The chromatic scale is basically the equivalent of our alphabet. Think of it as a never-ending number line. Once you reach the end of the line, you just start over at the beginning. You can also think of it circularly, imagining the notes as numbers on a clock.

Each step on the line, or around the clock, equals one fret on the banjo.

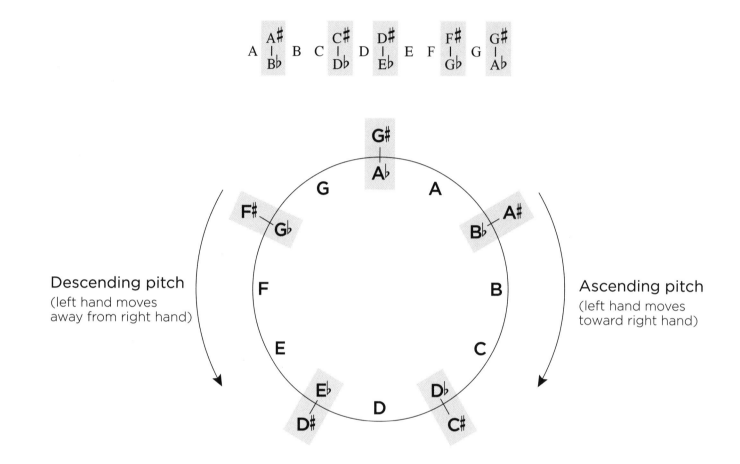

No matter where you start on the clock, to ascend (make the pitch higher), you follow the pattern around clockwise. If you're looking at the number line, you ascend left to right, as you move your left hand toward the right hand. Remember: one fret = one step on the clock or line.

No matter where you start on the clock, to descend (make the pitch lower), you follow the pattern around counter-clockwise. If you're looking at the number line, you descend right to left, as you move your left hand away from the right hand. Remember: one fret = one step on the clock or line.

Two Names?
You'll notice that some of the notes have two names. Both are equally correct, but you'll hear some names more commonly used. For instance, in bluegrass, we tend to say B♭, even though A♯ is equally valid.

SCOOTING THE CLOSED-POSITION CHORDS AROUND

Now, let's move around the chord shapes we just learned to play new chords. In fact, you are about to play every major chord on the banjo!

We'll start by ascending—i.e., making the pitch higher and moving the chord shape up the neck toward your right hand.

1. Make your F-shape G chord.

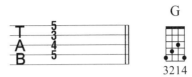

2. Now, find G on the number line or the clock. Maintaining the shape, move all your fingers up one fret—you just played a G♯ (or A♭) major chord!

3. Move it up again, and you're playing an A!

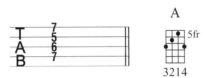

Do you see how this works? Starting with a chord you know—in this case, a G major—we can slide the shape around the neck to find any major chord we want.

Now, let's try descending—making the pitch lower by moving the shape down the neck, away from your right hand.

1. Go back to the starting shape—our F-shape G.

2. Now, find G on the number line or on the clock. Maintaining the shape, move all your fingers down (or back) a fret—you just played an F♯ (or G♭) major chord!

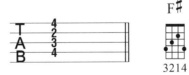

3. Move it down again, and you're playing an F!

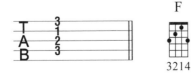

Do you see the value of this exercise? Once you memorize each of the three major chord shapes in G, you can slide them around to make any major chord you want, following the steps of the chromatic scale.

Notice that there are only 12 notes, or steps, before the scale repeats itself. Therefore, once you scoot your starting position up 12 frets, you've come full circle and gone G to G, etc.

Now that you've fingered closed-position chords and understand how to scoot them around on the neck, we can talk about *chopping*, or *vamping*. This is a commonly used backup technique. Though it may take some time to master, once you get the hang of chopping, it can easily be applied to any song.

Some people find they can apply this technique more quickly than low-rolling backup, while others prefer rolling. Regardless of your preference, the main goal is to be able to play some form of backup to every song you learn. Remember that when you play with other people, you'll spend more time backing others up than you will soloing.

CHOPPING WITH BASS STRING AND CHORDS

Let's start by making our F-shape G chord again.

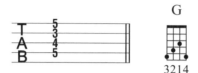

Hopefully, the fingering is a bit easier now and we can begin talking about the right hand, which creates the rhythmic and percussive nature we aim for while vamping. Our goal is to alternate a sustained downbeat (the sound continues to ring) on the bass string with a *staccato* chord on the upbeat. Staccato is indicated in the music by a dot above the notes, and it tells you to play the notes in a very short, clipped fashion (no sustain).

Whether a note sustains or not is determined by the amount of pressure used by the left hand. The sustained bass string will get a normal amount of pressure, like we've been using. We create the staccato upbeat by barely pressing on the strings. We want just enough pressure to hear the chord, but little enough so that the sound does not last long at all. The tricky part is balancing the two amounts of pressure: pressing hard on the bass string (sustaining) and pressing lightly on the higher strings (staccato). Simply identifying the sound you are aiming for will greatly help as you experiment to find what works best.

As for the right hand, it's fine to pull double-duty with our thumb by using it for the bass string and the following pinch.

Example 1

2:31

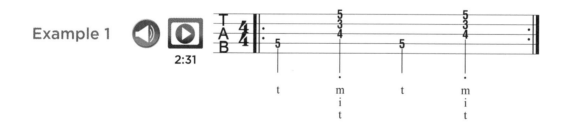

CHOPPING WITH CHORDS ONLY

If a song is too fast to play both the sustained bass string and staccato upbeat, or if it proves too challenging, our emphasis in chopping is the upbeat. Just leave out the sustained bass notes on the downbeats.

Example 2

CHOPPING BETWEEN THE F-SHAPE AND D-SHAPE G CHORDS

Remember the exercise in Lesson 7, where we slid the G chord between the F shape and D shape? We emphasized leaving the pinky and ring fingers down while we slid the shapes, so that the only fingers completely lifted were the middle and ring. They flip back and forth.

Now it's time to add the right hand to that exercise and practice chopping between the two positions.

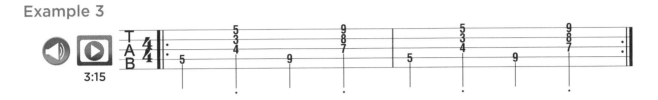

Example 3

CHOPPING TO "CRIPPLE CREEK"

Now, let's try chopping to "Cripple Creek." Though we could take one shape and slide it around, it would mean a lot of movement up and down the neck for very quick chord changes. That's why the previous exercise of transitioning between the F and D shapes is so valuable. This is the most efficient way to chop to the song "Cripple Creek." It uses a D-shape G chord, an F-shape C chord, and an F-shape D chord.

Note: Feel free to insert rests at the end of chopping if it helps you to get ready to start playing your solo again.

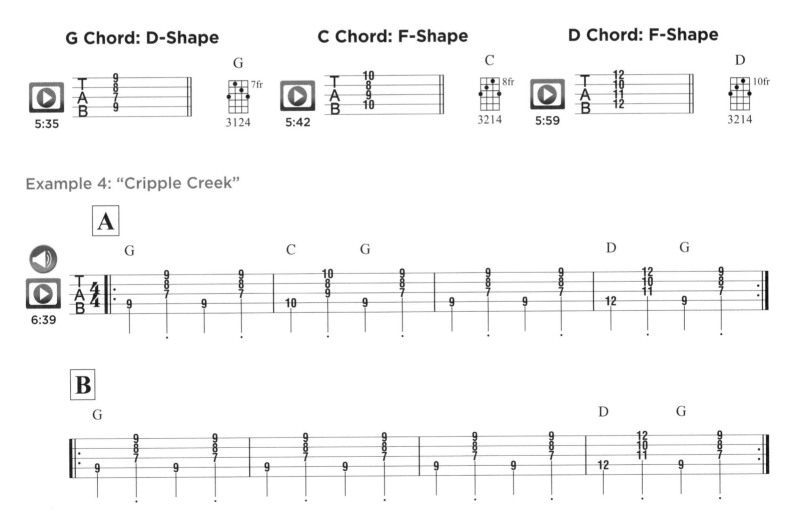

19

"BOIL THEM CABBAGE DOWN"

To be a complete banjo player, we need to be able to play lead and backup to each song, so we can accompany others and play solos. Congratulations! You have the skills to accomplish this! As a reward for the hard work in the previous chapters, let's combine everything we've learned to enjoy a song that has a relatively low difficulty level: "Boil Them Cabbage Down." There is no new content in this chapter. We're just assembling what we've learned to create a new song.

Below is a solo, two versions of low-rolling backup (remember you can mix and match the versions), and chopping backup. Enjoy!

For the solo, notice we use a measure of the alternating thumb roll followed by a measure of the forward/backward roll throughout. These are both rolls you learned early on.

> **Tip!**
> Did you know you can play the common 2-3 slide as a hammer-on if you prefer? Try it!

Example 1: Solo Version

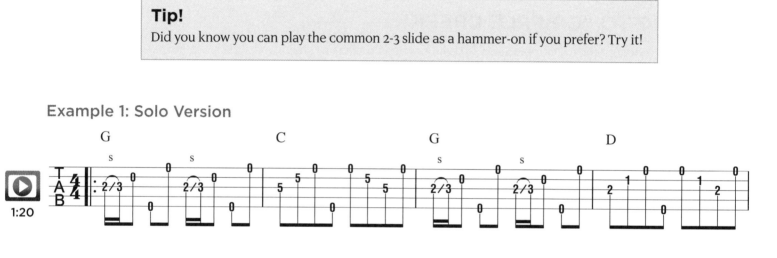

Example 2: Backup Version 1 – Alternating Thumb Roll

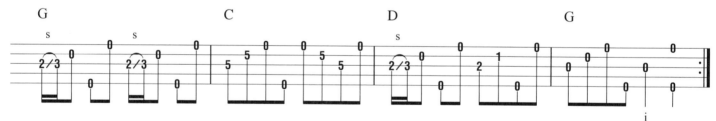

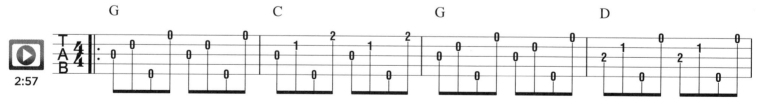

Example 3: Backup Version 2 – Forward/Backward Roll

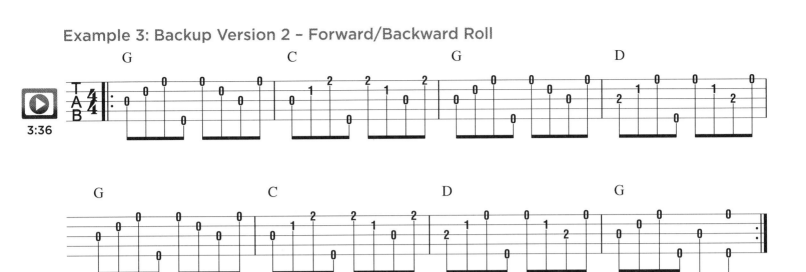

3:36

For the following chopping version of backup, we will use the D-shape G, F-shape C, and F-shape D positions. At the end, we see a new type of rest: a *half* rest. This lasts for half of a measure, or 2 beats, so it's twice as long as a quarter rest.

Example 4: Chopping Version

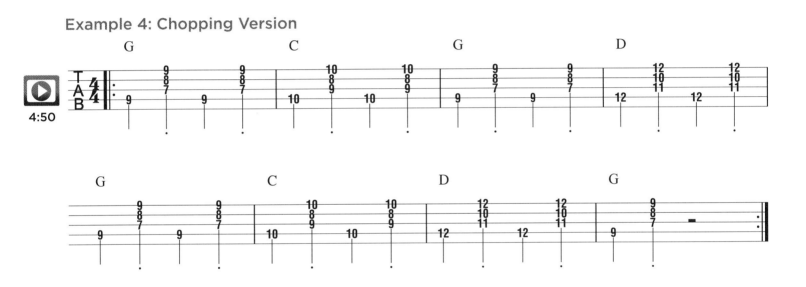

4:50

On this audio track, we will play the song five times with guitar. Try following this structure:

1. Solo (Example 1)
2. Alternating thumb backup (Example 2)
3. Forward/backward roll backup (Example 3)
4. Chopping backup (Example 4)
5. Solo again (Example 1)

Next, play the song three times through (solo-backup-solo) and let your backup section be a mixture—anything you choose. I played a mixture of the alternating thumb roll and the forward/backward roll on the demo track, but you can make your own decision. Remember, it's good to alter your roll right before the solo starts to help get ready to start the lead again.

Demo   Play-
        Along

1-2-1-5 ROLL

We are going to use the song "Old Joe Clark" to learn a new roll and a new chord. First, let's practice playing the 1-2-1-5 roll open.

Example 1

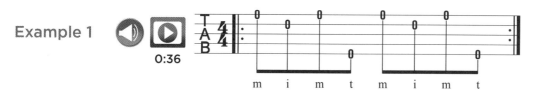

0:36

Now let's add the left hand to this roll, ending with a 1-2 pinch and open fifth string. We will often use a 1-2 pinch in this song. That's the only new skill you need to learn with your right hand for the solo!

Example 2

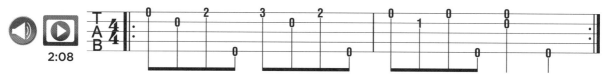

2:08

THE F CHORD

Now, let's talk about an F chord. Remember the chromatic scale that we talked about in Lesson 8? Refer back to pages 16-17 if you need to. Let's start with something we know, which is the F-shape G chord.

G Chord: F-Shape

2:55

F Chord: F-Shape

3:17

Let's try rolling the F chord with an alternating-thumb roll. Notice that we don't need to finger the fourth string, since the roll doesn't call for it, but we still use the left-hand fingers that would allow us to make the full-fingered chord.

Example 3

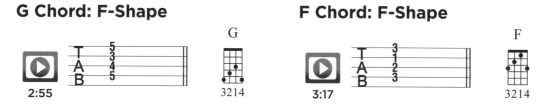

4:16

"OLD JOE CLARK"

Now you've conquered all the new material to play the solo to "Old Joe Clark!" Here's a solo version.

Example 4: Solo Version

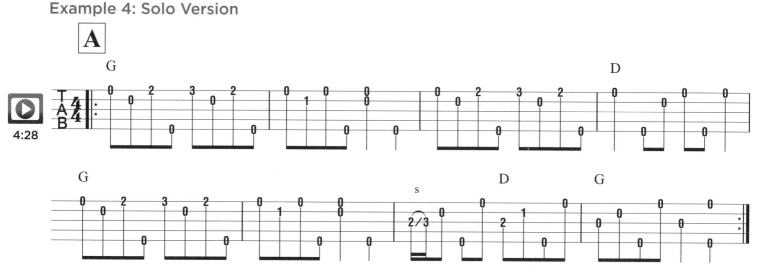

4:28

B

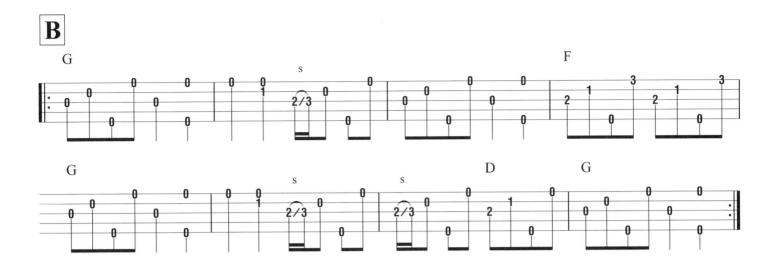

On the video, I play a low-rolling backup version that uses both the alternating thumb and forward/backward rolls to add variety. Following that is a chopping version to "Old Joe Clark." Remember: feel free to insert rests as needed at the end of backup to ensure we are ready to resume playing our solo.

We'll stick with our D-shape G, F-shape C, and F-shape D. We have a new chord position, however, when chopping. We will simply shift our D-shape G chord back two frets, just as we did with the F-shape, to create the F chord that we'll use for chopping.

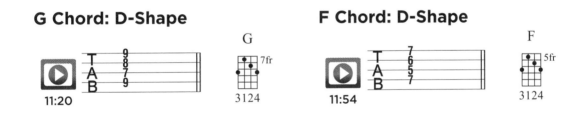

G Chord: D-Shape

11:20

F Chord: D-Shape

11:54

On this audio track, we play "Old Joe Clark" four times with guitar, using this structure:

1. Banjo solo (Example 4)

2. Rolling backup (Example 5)

3. Chopping (Example 6)

4. Solo again (Example 4)

Next, practice your backup and play three times through the song (solo-backup-solo). Remember that you can make your backup a mixture of everything you have learned so far.

Demo   Play-Along

 Each song we learn is an opportunity to build vocabulary. As a teacher, I can create a version of most any song that suits the student's playing level. A great way to build your vocabulary is through certain songs that repeat a new phrase. "When the Saints Go Marching In" gives us a wonderful opportunity to learn a common pickup-note phrase, as well as a common 2-3 hammer-on on our second string. At the end of the solo, we'll get a chance to learn one of the most played phrases we'll ever use: the famous "G-run." Let's look at these concepts individually, before we tackle the solo.

PICKUP NOTES

Pickup notes precede the downbeat of a song, usually at the beginning. In other words, pickup notes are what you often hear from the instrument starting the song prior to the rest of the band coming in. On banjo, the following passage is one of the most common ways we start a song. The band would come in on the first downbeat of the first full measure.

To play this phrase, we play three pinches on the first and second strings. This is usually done with our middle and index fingers, although you could substitute your thumb for the index on the second string if you prefer. On the left hand, there are a variety of ways to play this, but I'm going to suggest using your index finger on the first fret and then scooting it up to the second fret.

Example 1

1:27

THE SECOND-STRING 2-3 HAMMER-ON

Again, we have a very commonly used technique with our next skill. The second-string 2-3 hammer-on is a vital part of bluegrass banjo playing. We will build on it later, but for now, let's do a single hammer-on on the second string.

Example 2

3:01

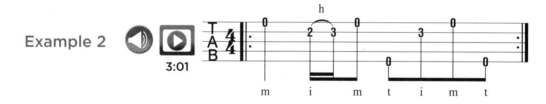

THE G-RUN

Guitar G-Run

Once you learn this lick and can identify it, you will hear it over and over (at least in bluegrass music). I call it the "G-run" because it mimics the guitar phrase with the same name. I'll play it on guitar, so you can hear the equivalent.

This is a challenging sequence. I am going to write two different right-hand fingerings because sometimes we start the phrase with our thumb—other times, with our index. There is also a variation that starts with a quarter note rather than two eighth notes. These two phrases are interchangeable.

I cannot emphasize enough how important it is to master the G-run! You will play some form of it in virtually every song, and it's crucial to play it correctly and automatically. When I say "G-run," I expect the phrase to just fall out of students.

Pay special attention to the right-hand fingering. In Example 3, you can't double a finger because eighth notes don't give you enough time, so avoid the common mistake of letting your thumb play strings back to back. Notice in Example 4, however, we begin with a quarter note, allowing us time to play both the beginning third string and the following fifth string with the thumb.

> **Tip!**
> You may prefer to slide instead of hammer-on. Both are acceptable. Use your middle finger if you choose to slide.

Example 3

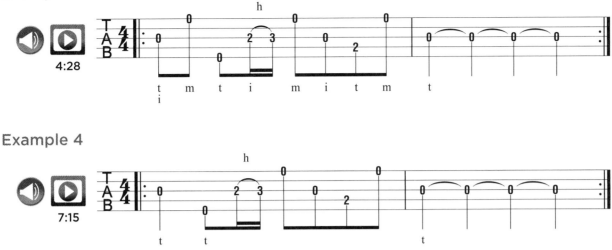

Example 4

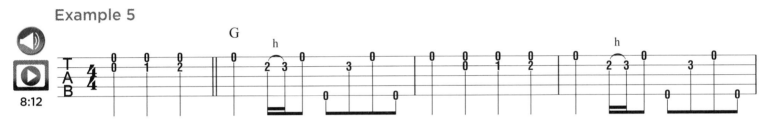

"WHEN THE SAINTS GO MARCHING IN"

Now, we are ready to play the song "When the Saints Go Marching In" using all these techniques. In measure 10, note that the pattern is a forward roll, not an alternating thumb roll.

Example 5

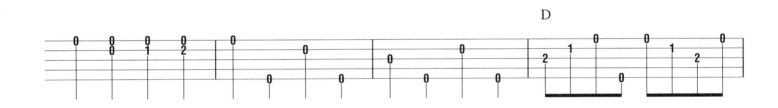

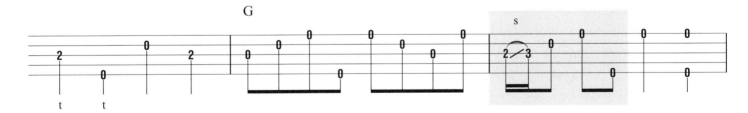

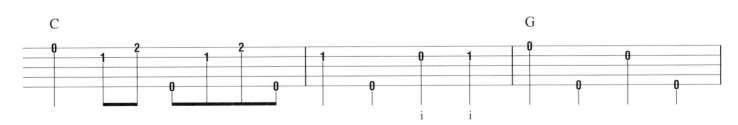

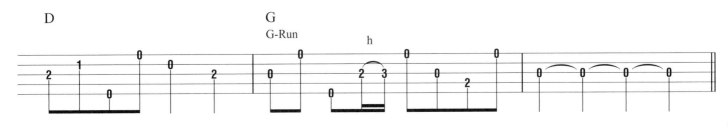

 Throughout "When the Saints Go Marching In," you'll notice that I play the lead pickup notes on the banjo for each of the audio tracks, even though it's not notated. This is just to help you know when to come in. You would normally not play these pickup notes unless you were about to start a solo.

Example 1: Chopping Version

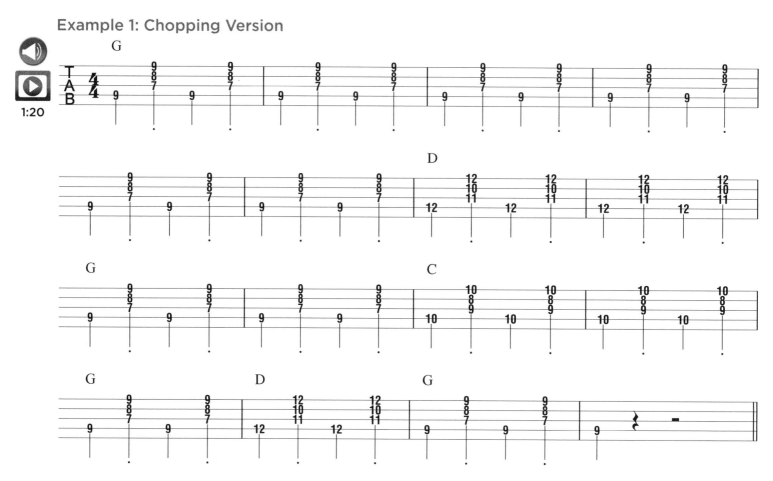

Let's start with a version that utilizes both alternating thumb and forward/backward rolls to help provide some variety. The alternating thumb rolls are shaded to help you tell them apart.

Example 2: Low-Rolling Version 1

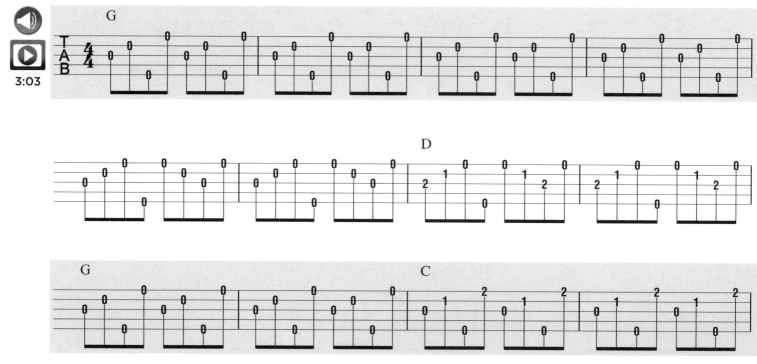

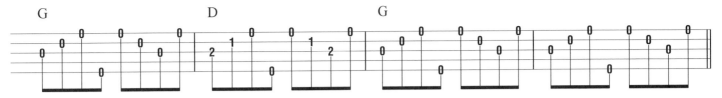

ADDING VARIETY TO THE LOW-ROLLING BACKUP

Now let's add even more variety in our low-rolling backup. By making subtle changes, we can create different sounds. The difficulty won't necessarily increase. For instance, with our typical 3-2-5-1 alternating thumb roll, we may follow it up with a similar roll, but use 4-2-5-1 instead so that the fourth string is incorporated. The fourth string is shaded to help you identify the 4-2-5-1 sequences. Also, our G-run is a wonderful phrase to use in backup. We'll end this version of backup with the G-run in the next-to-last measure. We're also going to insert a common walk-up on the fourth string. Again, the quarter notes are what allow us time to use our thumb for each of the notes. Here's the walk-up phrase:

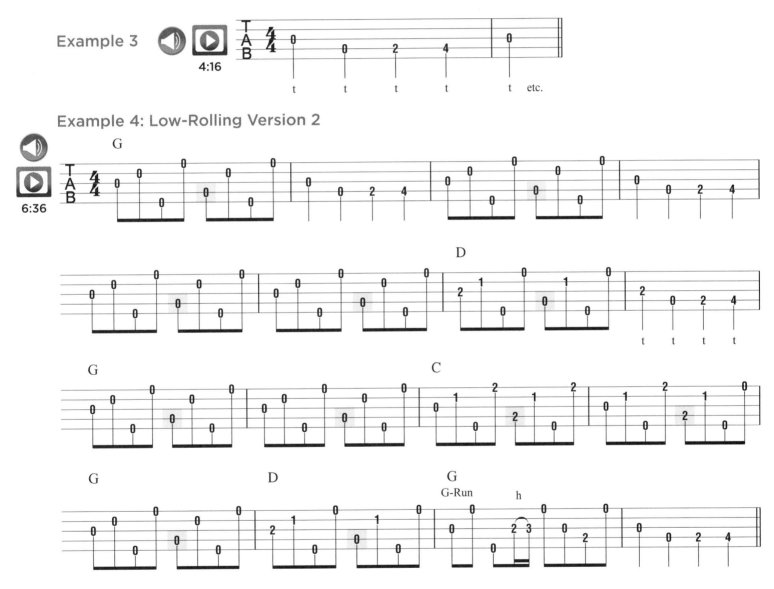

It's time for our whole band version for this song. Just as before, I am going to mix up the backup by playing rolls during the first half and chopping on the second half. It's very important to remember that this song has pickup notes that require a lot of preparation, so be ready for your solo! Notice at the end of the first solo that I added the walk-up on the fourth string (Example 3) to lead us into the backup.

In this track, we'll play "When the Saints Go Marching In" three times, using the following structure:

Demo

1. Solo (see Lesson 12, Example 6)

2. Backup (mixing low-rolling and chopping styles)

Play-Along

3. Solo again

 One of the most common rolls you will hear in bluegrass banjo is one I refer to as the "Foggy Mountain Breakdown" roll. It incorporates two hammer-ons on the second string followed by a forward roll. In fact, you may recognize the following Example 1 as the beginning snippet to that song.

One of the first things to discuss is right-hand fingering. We have established that, unless we are playing quarter notes (or longer) that allow us enough time, we do not typically double a finger on the right hand. As long as you abide by that rule, you are presumably safe.

"FOGGY MOUNTAIN BREAKDOWN" ROLL

For an unknown reason, Earl Scruggs' right-hand fingering of this roll is unorthodox. He dropped his thumb down to the second string without being required to, considering the rule we just talked about. In short, it is completely acceptable to use the more predictable index finger instead of our thumb for the first two times we strike the second string. However, since Scruggs was such a master player, who established the rule book that most of us still follow today, I believe that trying his way is warranted. The first note of beat 2 uses his thumb fingering.

Example 1

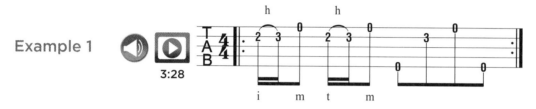

Here's the same passage fingered with the index on the second string both times. As the audio clips will demonstrate, there is little to no difference in sound, so I don't believe using the thumb is required. Being able to readily use any finger on any string, however, is valuable, so if you can equip yourself to drop your thumb down to the second string, it will be beneficial in the long run.

Example 2

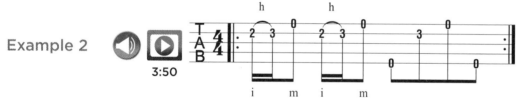

Now let's change the last part of the passage by altering the forward roll. Instead of using the second string, let's play a pull-off on the third string. Pay special attention to how the index is used to play the third string; this avoids doubling the thumb, which has just been used on the fifth string.

Example 3

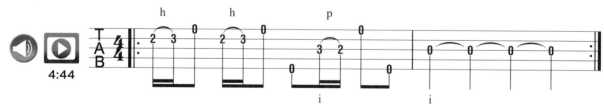

Now let's discover the opening snippet to the song "Foggy Mountain Breakdown" with what we have learned above. This passage begins with Example 1 played two times, followed by Example 3.

Example 4

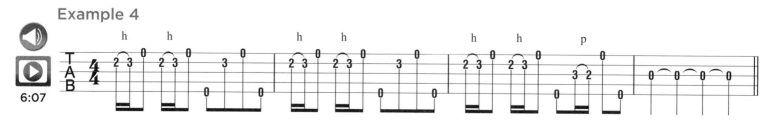

"OH! SUSANNA"

Roll

Now, let's apply the "Foggy Mountain Breakdown" roll (Example 1) to a song. The roll isn't just available to us in this one context. We can use it in a variety of chords and contexts. Following, we have the lead solo to the song "Oh! Susanna." The roll (shaded) is the first part of the chorus and it is played over a C chord in the position you have played many times. But then we move to a higher C chord, using a barre-shape on the fifth fret. Listen to the audio track to hear this section by itself.

Also, pay special attention to which rolls are alternating thumb (3-2-5-1) and which are forward (3-2-1-5). Confusing those two rolls seems to be the biggest obstacle for folks on this song.

Example 5

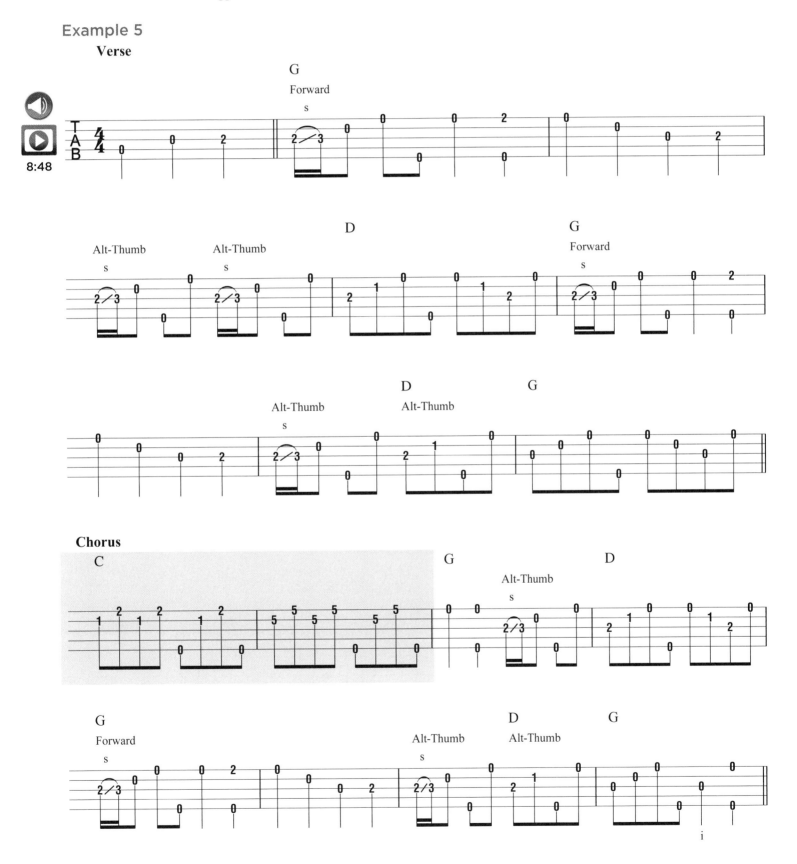

 Now let's focus on playing more varied backup using all the skills we have acquired.

First, let's chop through the song "Oh! Susanna." As with the last song, I played the lead pickup notes, even though they're not notated, just to help us know where to come in.

Example 1: Chopping Version

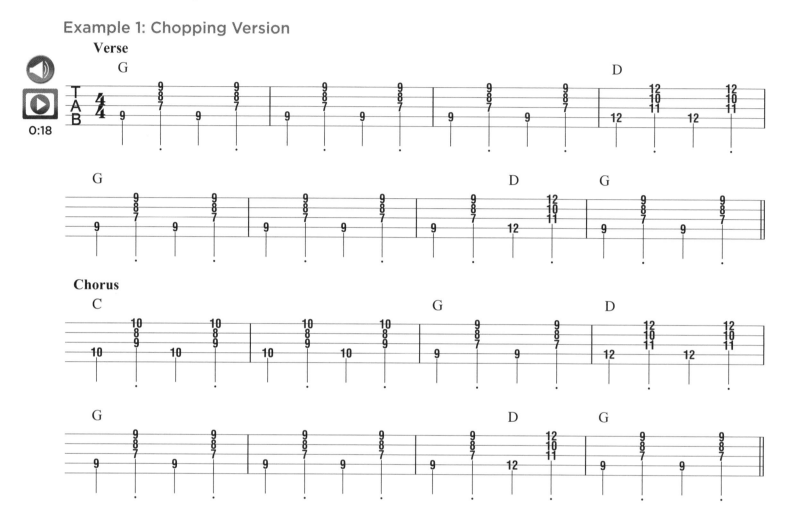

Now for low-rolling backup, let's incorporate lots of our skills. Varied alternating thumb rolls that incorporate the fourth string, pinches to break up the constant eighth-note roll patterns, and forward/backward rolls are all used to give us a variety of sounds. This is a nice culmination for all of your hard work.

Example 2: Low-Rolling Version

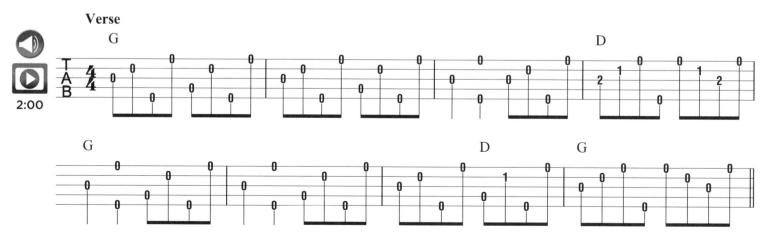

Chorus

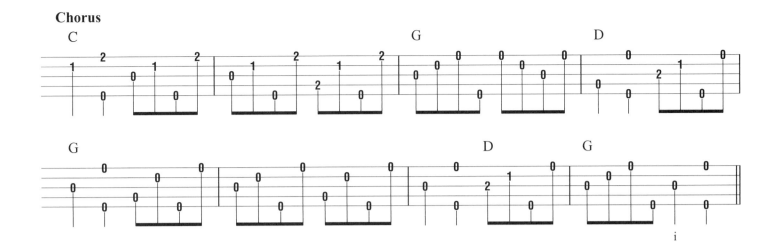

ENDING

For the final skill, I thought we should learn an ending. For now, simply tack this on to the end of any song. This phrase is commonly referred to as "shave and a haircut." Everyone seems to enjoy adding this to their vocabulary. Check out the Conclusion video to see this example demonstrated. And don't forget to play it at the end of the following audio tracks, which allow you to play solo, backup, solo, and ending!

Those of you who listen intently will notice a slide at the end of the first measure. Scruggs did this all the time; he let us hear the transitions of the left hand. We have to go all the way from the seventh fret on the third string to the 16th fret of the first string. Why not let our slide be heard? Our hand has to make the journey anyway. The slide isn't imperative, so don't feel as though you have to do it, but if it's natural to you, let your left-hand transition be heard.

Example 3

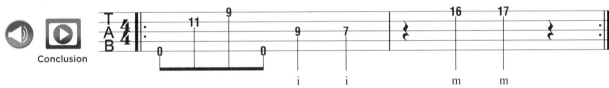

Conclusion

"OH! SUSANNA"

Demo

Now, we have whole band clips again played solo-backup-solo to let you practice your skills with lead, varied backup (I chose low-rolling backup with alternating thumb and forward/backward rolls on the verse, and chopping on the chorus), and an ending. You have become a complete banjo player on these songs!

Play-Along

The "Oh! Susanna" banjo solo is Example 5 from Lesson 14.

AFTERWORD

Congratulations on making it to the end of the book. We have learned so much—from how to hold and tune your banjo, to playing various lead and backup parts to several songs.

While I'm delighted to have the opportunity to work with you through this book, I highly recommend also seeking time with a private teacher. Beware, though! An ill-equipped teacher can do more harm than good, so do your research and try to locate a musician who is firmly rooted in the Scruggs-style fundamentals. With online lessons being readily available, finding a wonderful player and teacher is easier than ever.

I also encourage you to find local jam sessions and/or bluegrass festivals. Music really comes alive when it's shared with other people. With the whole band tracks, we have done our best to simulate a live music setting, but there is no substitute for playing with other musicians.

Finally, tab is a great tool, but unlike some genres, bluegrass music isn't meant to be read. So use the tab to learn, but then try to detach from it and just play the song.

Good luck,
Kristin

 Bonus Track! Consider the last audio track a bonus track—something to which you can aspire! I'm playing many of the things we covered in this book (among other things), but just at a faster tempo.